All About

CLIMATE MAPS

- ⬤ POLAR ZONE
- ⬤ COLD ZONE
- ⬤ TEMPERATE ZONE
- ⬤ DRY ZONE
- ⬤ TROPICAL ZONE

PACIFIC OCEAN

ATLANTIC OCEAN

INDIAN OCEAN

ARCTIC OCEAN

By Barbara M. Linde

Gareth Stevens
PUBLISHING

Please visit our website, www.garethstevens.com. For a free color catalog of all our high-quality books, call toll free 1-800-542-2595 or fax 1-877-542-2596.

Cataloging-in-Publication Data

Names: Linde, Barbara M.
Title: All about climate maps / Barbara M. Linde.
Description: New York : Gareth Stevens Publishing, 2019. | Series: Map basics | Includes glossary and index.
Identifiers: ISBN 9781538232606 (pbk.) | ISBN 9781538229156 (library bound) | ISBN 9781538232613 (6pack)
Subjects: LCSH: Maps–Juvenile literature. | Weather–Maps–Juvenile literature.
Classification: LCC GA105.6 L56 2019 | DDC 912.01'4–dc23

First Edition

Published in 2019 by
Gareth Stevens Publishing
111 East 14th Street, Suite 349
New York, NY 10003

Copyright © 2019 Gareth Stevens Publishing

Designer: Sarah Liddell
Editor: Monika Davies

Photo credits: Cover, pp. 1, 9 trgrowth/Shutterstock.com; p. 5 Patrick Foto/Shutterstock.com; pp. 7, 15, 19 ekler/Shutterstock.com; p. 11 photo courtesy of the NOAA; p. 13 Bluegleam/Wikimedia Commons; p. 17 Carnby/Wikimedia Commons; p. 20 Wolkenengel565/Shutterstock.com.

Printed in the United States of America

CPSIA compliance information: Batch #CW19GS: For further information contact Gareth Stevens, New York, New York at 1-800-542-2595.

CONTENTS

Words in the glossary appear in **bold** type the first time they are used in the text.

HOW ARE CLIMATE AND WEATHER DIFFERENT?

If you say, "It's 90 degrees and cloudy today," you're talking about the weather. Weather is what the **temperature** and other outdoor conditions are like at a certain point in time. Weather can change day to day—or even minute to minute—depending on conditions in the **atmosphere** at any given time.

If you say, "It's usually warm and rainy here in

JUST THE FACTS
Scientists studying the climate of an area will record and measure the average weather over a 30-year period.

July," you're talking about climate. Climate is what the **average** weather conditions are like in a place over a long period of time.

4

Weather can change quickly! You might notice that it's sunny in the morning but rainy and cloudy in the afternoon.

5

WHAT ARE CLIMATE MAPS?

Maps are drawings that give information about a place. Climate maps show information about the average climate conditions over a month-long or year-long period. Different weather conditions—such as temperature, **precipitation**, and wind—are some parts of the climate.

Climate maps usually give information about only one climatic condition. Some climate maps give information about small areas, such as a city. Others show a larger area, such as the whole world. The **legend** on a climate map explains how to read the map.

JUST THE FACTS

Some maps include a compass rose. This is a circular **symbol** that shows the different directions: north, south, east, and west.

6

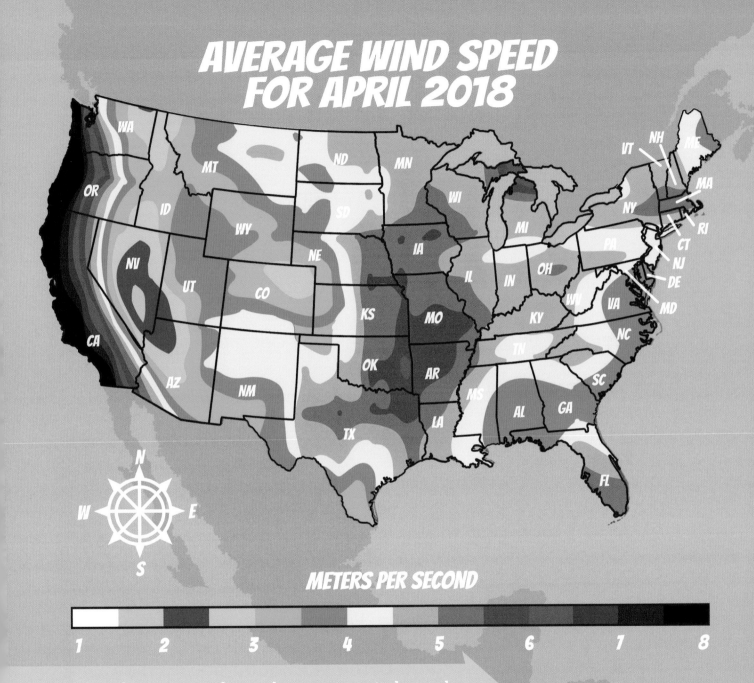

AVERAGE WIND SPEED FOR APRIL 2018

METERS PER SECOND

1 2 3 4 5 6 7 8

This climate map shows the average wind speed throughout the United States in April 2018. The legend shows how fast the wind blew in meters per second. One meter is equal to a little more than 3 feet.

CLIMATE ZONES MAPS

Using the Köppen climate **classification** system, Earth's climate can be grouped into five main zones: tropical, dry, temperate, cold, and polar. Tropical zones are very hot and rainy. Dry zones don't get much rain, and the temperature often changes greatly from day to night.

Temperate zones have mild climates that aren't too hot or too cold. Cold zones stay cold for many months and may get a lot of snow and ice. Polar zones—the coldest areas on Earth—are located at the North and South Poles.

JUST THE FACTS

In 1900, Wladimir Köppen designed a system of climate classification. Today, it's one of the most widely used systems to classify climate.

KÖPPEN'S WORLD CLIMATES

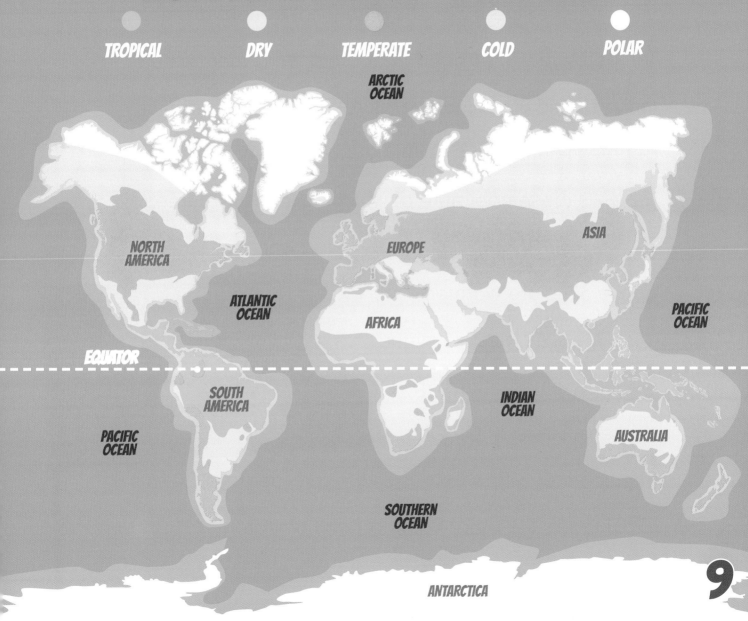

TROPICAL   DRY   TEMPERATE   COLD   POLAR

ARCTIC OCEAN

NORTH AMERICA

EUROPE

ASIA

ATLANTIC OCEAN

AFRICA

PACIFIC OCEAN

EQUATOR

SOUTH AMERICA

INDIAN OCEAN

AUSTRALIA

PACIFIC OCEAN

SOUTHERN OCEAN

ANTARCTICA

TEMPERATURE MAPS

Temperature maps show how hot or cold a place is. Temperature is measured in degrees on a thermometer. In the United States, temperature is often measured in degrees Fahrenheit (°F). Thirty-two degrees Fahrenheit (32°F) is the temperature at which water usually freezes. Temperatures below 32°F are colder, while temperatures above 32°F are warmer.

However, most countries measure temperatures in degrees Celsius (°C). On a thermometer with a Celsius scale, zero degrees Celsius (0°C) marks the usual freezing point of water.

JUST THE FACTS
Global temperatures are rising. This is because there are more of certain types of gases around Earth. These gases trap heat, which cause the world's climate to grow warmer.

TEMPERATURE MAP FOR MARCH 2018

AVERAGE TEMPERATURE (°F)

0   50   100

This climate map shows the average temperatures in the United States for March 2018. On the legend, dark blue stands for 0°F (-17°C), while dark red stands for 100°F (37.7°C) temperatures.

RAINFALL MAPS

Rainfall maps show the average amount of precipitation that falls in a place over a period of time. Some rainfall maps show the average precipitation over many years.

This rainfall map shows the state of Oregon on the West Coast of the United

States. The Cascade Mountains divide the state from north to south. The Pacific Ocean brings a lot of rain to the western part of the state. Most of the rain doesn't reach over the mountains, so eastern Oregon is much drier than western Oregon.

RAINFALL MAP OF OREGON

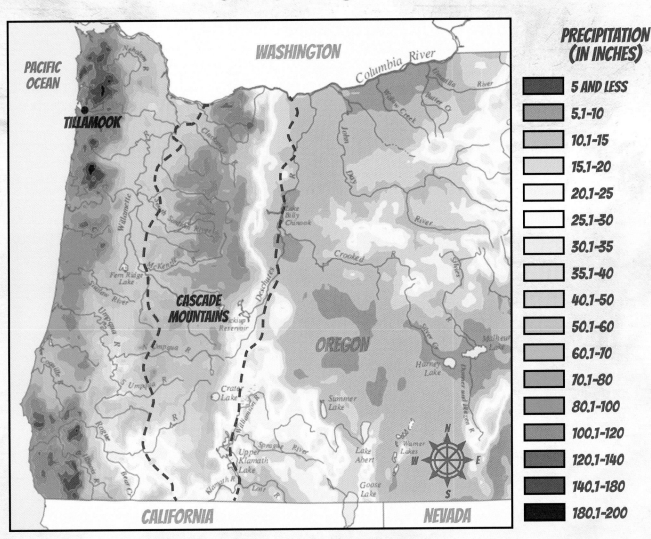

PRECIPITATION (IN INCHES)

- 5 AND LESS
- 5.1-10
- 10.1-15
- 15.1-20
- 20.1-25
- 25.1-30
- 30.1-35
- 35.1-40
- 40.1-50
- 50.1-60
- 60.1-70
- 70.1-80
- 80.1-100
- 100.1-120
- 120.1-140
- 140.1-180
- 180.1-200

This rainfall map shows the average amount precipitation that fell in Oregon from 1961 to 1990. Notice how the Cascade Mountains stop much of the rain from reaching the eastern side of the state.

PRECIPITATION OUTLOOK MAPS

Is it going to rain soon? A precipitation **outlook** map might answer your question. To create a precipitation outlook map, scientists ask, "What's going on in the atmosphere and ocean?" They also see if there's been precipitation in the area lately. Their answers help them **predict** how much precipitation will fall in the future.

Scientists also use precipitation outlook maps to predict which places will likely get more or less precipitation than usual.

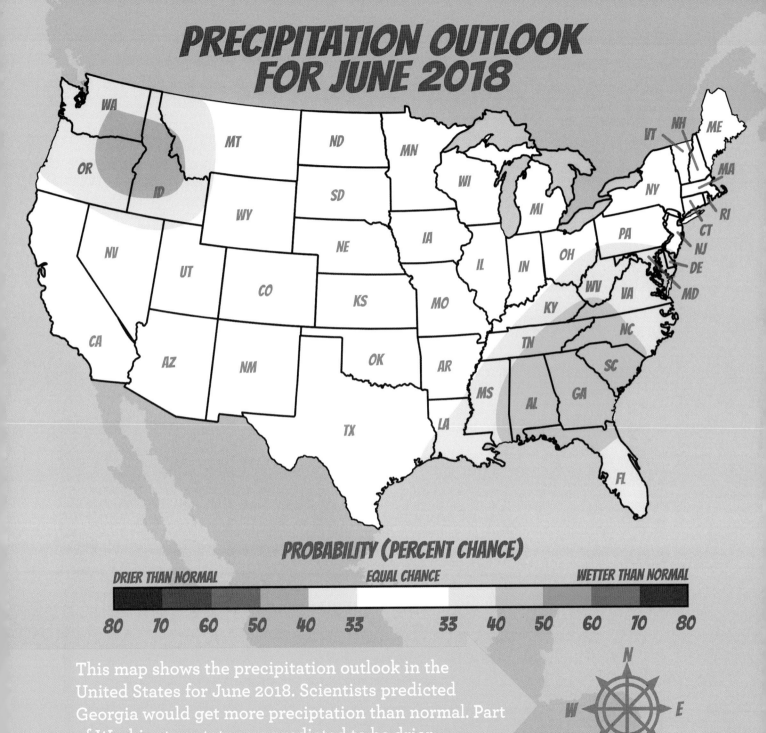

PRECIPITATION OUTLOOK FOR JUNE 2018

PROBABILITY (PERCENT CHANCE)

DRIER THAN NORMAL — EQUAL CHANCE — WETTER THAN NORMAL

80 70 60 50 40 33   33 40 50 60 70 80

This map shows the precipitation outlook in the United States for June 2018. Scientists predicted Georgia would get more precipitation than normal. Part of Washington state was predicted to be drier than usual.

15

GLOBAL SUNSHINE MAPS

Sunshine is a part of climate, too. The light from the sun warms Earth's land and water. The amount of sunshine a place gets is important to farmers, gardeners, builders, and other workers. People planning to move or go on a vacation might check for the sunniest places.

This map shows how many hours of sunshine different areas of the world receive. Northern Africa gets many hours of sunshine, while Antarctica gets very few hours of sunshine!

JUST THE FACTS

The sunniest city in the United States is Yuma, Arizona. The US city that gets the least amount of sunshine is Juneau, Alaska.

On this sunshine map, areas with yellow, orange, or red shading receive lots of sun, while areas with dark purple shading get very few hours of sunshine.

WORLD YEARLY SUNSHINE HOURS

LESS THAN 1200 HOURS **1200-1600 HOURS** **1600-2000 HOURS** **2000-2400 HOURS** **2400-3000 HOURS** **3000-3600 HOURS** **3600-4000 HOURS** **MORE THAN 4000 HOURS**

ARCTIC OCEAN

NORTH AMERICA

ASIA

EUROPE

ATLANTIC OCEAN

PACIFIC OCEAN

PACIFIC OCEAN

SOUTH AMERICA

AFRICA

INDIAN OCEAN

AUSTRALIA

N

W · E

S

SOUTHERN OCEAN

ANTARCTICA

COMPARING CLIMATE MAPS

Plants and trees that produce fruit and nuts need a certain number of chilling hours in a year to grow. Chilling hours happen when the temperature is between 32°F (0°C) and 45°F (7.2°C) in the winter.

These four maps show chilling hours in California

between 1950 and 2090. The first two maps show the past number of chilling hours recorded in California. The second two maps show how many chilling hours scientists think there will be if the climate continues to get warmer.

WINTER CHILLING HOURS IN CALIFORNIA

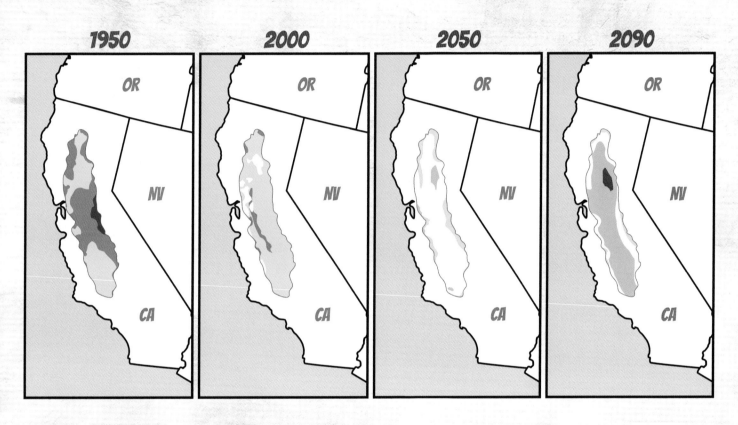

1950   2000   2050   2090

CHILLING HOURS

0-250   251-500   501-750   751-1,000   1,001-1,250   1,251-1,500

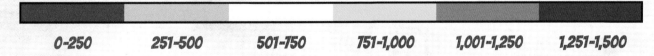

If the number of chilling hours in California continues to go down, farmers may have to plant different crops or plant in different areas.

MAP IT!

In the United States, each state can experience very different weather. Some states are dry and sunny all year long, while others get lots of rain.

Do you know how much precipitation falls in your home state? Complete online **research** and use books and newspapers to find out more about your state's precipitation levels. Then, design your own rainfall map! Once you've finished your map, share your it with your classmates. Are your maps similar or different?

MAKE A RAINFALL MAP!

1 WHAT ARE FIVE BIG CITIES IN YOUR HOME STATE? WRITE DOWN THEIR NAMES.

2 LOOK UP THE AVERAGE PRECIPITATION IN EACH CITY. RECORD THE PRECIPITATION LEVELS BESIDE EACH CITY'S NAME. ARE THE PRECIPITATION LEVELS SIMILAR OR DIFFERENT THAN EACH OTHER?

3 PRINT A BLANK MAP OF YOUR STATE. LABEL THE FIVE CITIES.

4 FIND FIVE DIFFERENT-COLORED PENS OR PENCILS. CHOOSE COLORS TO REPRESENT THE AMOUNT OF RAINFALL IN EACH CITY.

5 COLOR IN YOUR STATE'S RAINFALL MAP. THEN, CREATE A LEGEND THAT EXPLAINS WHAT EACH COLOR ON YOUR MAP MEANS.

GLOSSARY

atmosphere: the mixture of gases that surround a planet

average: a number that is calculated by adding quantities together and then dividing the total by the number of quantities

classification: the assignment of something to a category or class based on shared qualities

legend: a list that explains the symbols on a map

outlook: a set of conditions that will probably exist in the future

precipitation: rain, snow, sleet, or hail

predict: to guess what will happen in the future based on facts or knowledge

research: studying to find something new

symbol: a picture, shape, or object that stands for something else

temperature: how hot or cold something is

FOR MORE INFORMATION

BOOKS

Hirsch, Rebecca. *Using Climate Maps.* Minneapolis, MN: Lerner Publications, 2017.

Maloof, Torrey. *Climate.* Huntington Beach, CA: Teacher Created Materials, 2015.

O'Brien, Cynthia. *Climate Maps.* New York, NY: Crabtree Publishing, 2013.

WEBSITES

A Student's Guide to Global Climate Change
www3.epa.gov/climatechange//kids/index.html
Learn the basics about climate change and its impact on Earth. Then, learn how to be part of the solution to reduce climate change!

Climate.gov Data Snapshots
climate.gov/maps-data/data-snapshots/start
Check out NOAA's collection of current and past US climate maps, featuring precipitation outlooks, average temperatures, and more.

NASA Climate Kids
climatekids.nasa.gov/menu/weather-and-climate
Discover NASA's collection of online games, activities, and videos to learn more about climate!

INDEX